PLAYING BAR CHORDS

BY RON CENTOLA

To Jennifer and Mark

Technical Photos by Alan Packard

INTRODUCTION

This method was developed after years of teaching students of all ages. The greater part of this book focuses on the playing of bar chords. This is not a list of chords, but a step by step, easy to follow method for mastering the bar chord. This book allows the student to build from the playing and mastering of small bar chords to the playing and mastering of full bar chords.

There are also two special sections at the end of the book of interest to all guitar students. A chart has been developed which makes it very easy for a student with no knowledge of music theory to change the chords of a song to fit his voice (change the key).

A second chart has been developed which shows you how to figure out the chords of songs that you want to play by simply listening to those songs (playing by ear).

I hope the new ideas and approaches in this book bring you a great deal of musical enjoyment.

Ron Centola

SPECIAL FEATURES

1) Important points to remember are in bold print.

2) Instructions are set out in a point by point form.

3) A method is provided enabling you to build from simple bar chords to complete bar chords with plenty of practice at each step.

4) A section is devoted to showing the student how to change the chords of a song to fit his or her voice.

5) A technique has been developed making it easy for you to figure out the chords to popular songs that you want to learn.

6) A method is provided making it easy for you to learn how to play rock progressions using full bar chords.

7) An explanation is given for the reason why the names of chords change as you move them up and down the neck of the guitar.

TABLE OF CONTENTS

LIST OF SONGS (RHYTHMS)

BEGINNING BAR POSITION

A bar chord is a chord which **requires you to press down on more than one string at the same time** with one or more fingers.

The symbol for a bar chord is either ①–① or ①① The number inside the circle indicates the finger you should use to play the bar. These signs indicate that you must press down on two strings with the 1st finger. (The position of this symbol on a guitar diagram determines what strings and what fret you should play).

We will start by placing the beginning bar position on the 5th fret. (We are starting on the 5th fret because bar positions are usually easier to play on the middle frets).

To play this position you must **press down** on the **5th fret of the 1st string** and on the **5th fret of the 2nd string with your 1st finger. Only play** the **1st** and **2nd strings.**

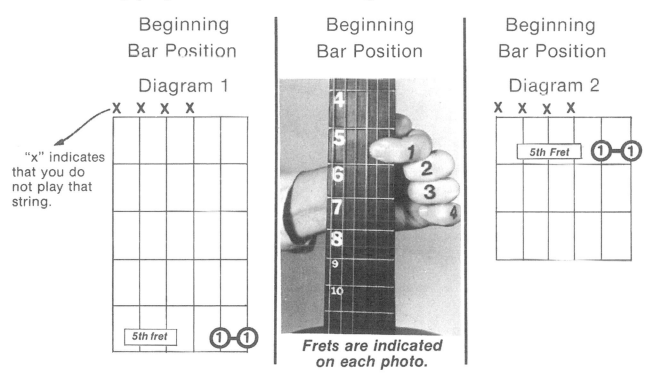

Beginning Bar Position Diagram 1

"x" indicates that you do not play that string.

5th fret ①–①

Beginning Bar Position

Frets are indicated on each photo.

Beginning Bar Position Diagram 2

5th Fret ①–①

Both diagram 1 and diagram 2 represent the same position on the guitar (5th fret). For the sake of saving space, the diagrams in this book will be drawn like diagram 2. In other words, the fret number where the chord begins will be indicated on the diagram.

Practice this beginning bar position until both the 1st and 2nd strings make a clear sound.

Three Ways Of Playing The Beginning Bar Positions

Here are three ways to play the beginning bar position. Choose the one that is the most comfortable for you. Remember, once you place your 1st finger in the 1st bar position, you should be able to play the 1st and 2nd strings and get two clear sounds on any fret of the guitar.

Example 1

1) Press straight down on the strings. Your thumb should be pressing firmly on the back center of the guitar.

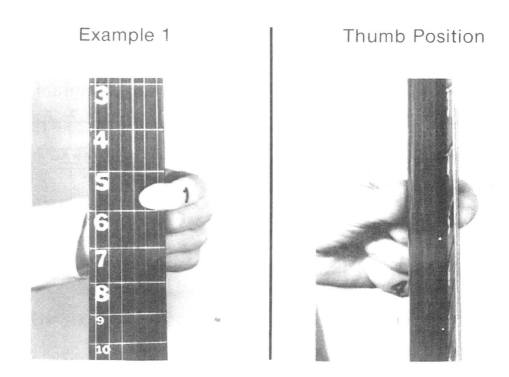

Example 1 | Thumb Position

This is the correct use of the thumb and should be used for all bar chord positions.

Example Number 2

Roll your finger backwards slightly.

Example Number 2

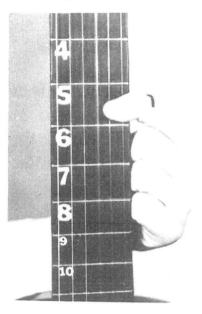

Example Number 3

Roll your finger slightly forward.

Example Number 3

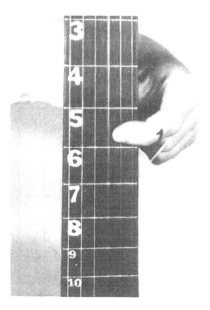

Remember to press your thumb firmly on the back center of the neck of the guitar.

EL 2803

SOME THINGS TO LEARN
PLAYING BAR CHORDS

Flats

You must also know how to flat a note on the guitar.

1) This is a flat sign ♭.

GENERAL RULE

To **flat a note** on the guitar you must **move the note down one fret** (towards the top of the guitar) and **stay on the same string.** (examples follow). The position of the natural notes will be enclosed in a circle and the flated notes in a rectangle.

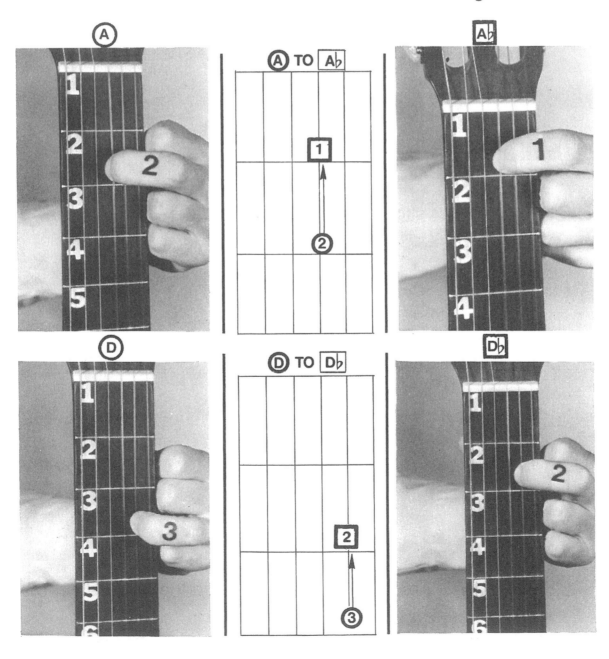

Sharps

Before we begin with actual bar chords, we must learn how to sharp on the guitar.

1) This is a sharp sign ♯.

GENERAL RULE

1) To sharp a note on the guitar you **move the note up one fret** (towards the hole of your guitar) and **remain on the same string.** (examples follow). The position of the natural note will be enclosed in a circle and the sharped note in a rectangle.

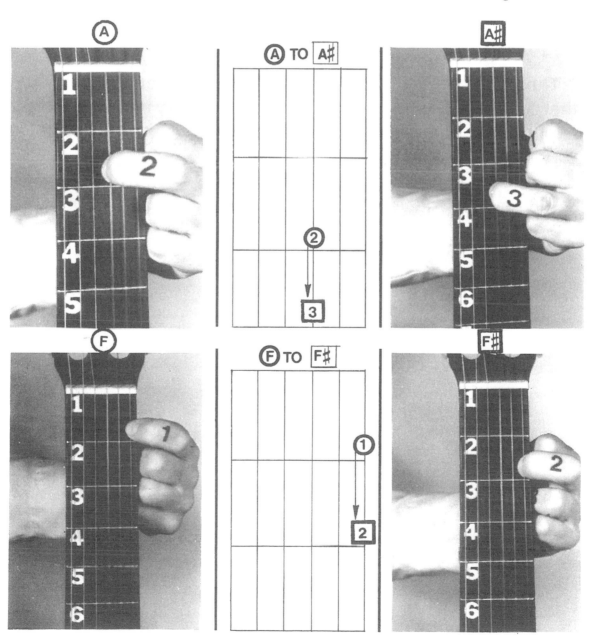

The Musical Alphabet

It is extremely important that you understand the musical alphabet if you are to understand bar chords.

There are two major differences between the musical alphabet and the regular alphabet.

Difference Number 1

A comes after G in the musical alphabet.

A B C D E F G A B C D E F G A etc.

The musical alphabet repeats itself over and over again. The fact that A follows G in the musical alphabet is a very important rule to remember. In the pages to follow your knowledge of this rule will be very helpful.

Student Notes

_____

Difference Number 2

We will spend a good deal of time on difference number 2 because it can be confusing.

The musical alphabet has sharps and flats between some of its letters.

Remember this is a sharp sign - ♯

This is a flat sign - ♭

Here is the musical alphabet with the sharps and flats added.

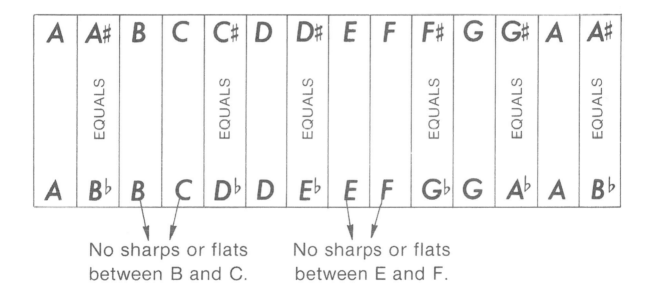

No sharps or flats between B and C.

No sharps or flats between E and F.

You must be wondering how A♯ (sharp) can be the same as B♭ (flat). Actually, these two signs represent the same note. This is explained in detail on the next page.

How Flats Can Also Be Sharps
And Sharps Can Also Be Flats

Every flat is also **a sharp** and **every sharp is** also **a flat.**

Example 1   *Example 2*

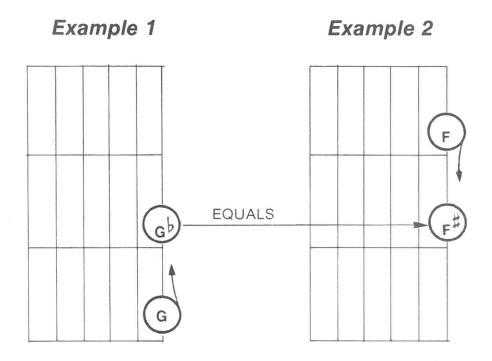

In example 1 we started with a G note. We took G and moved it from the 3rd fret, 1st string to the 2nd fret, 1st string. Moving the note back one fret makes it flat. G♭(flat) is on the 2nd fret, 1st string. G and G♭ are two separate notes.

In example 2 we started with an F note. We moved the F up one fret from the 1st fret, 1st string to the 2nd fret, 1st string. Moving the note forward one fret makes it sharp. F♯ (sharp) is on the 2nd fret, 1st string. F and F♯ are also two separate notes.

G♭ is on the 2nd fret, 1st string. (Look at example 1)

F♯ is also on the 2nd fret, 1st string. (Look at example 2)

Conclusion

G♭ and F♯ must be the **same note** because **they are on the exact same position of the guitar.** (2nd fret of the 1st string) G♭ and F♯ are the same note with different names.

How Flats Can Also Be Sharps
And Sharps Can Also Be Flats

Example 3   *Example 4*

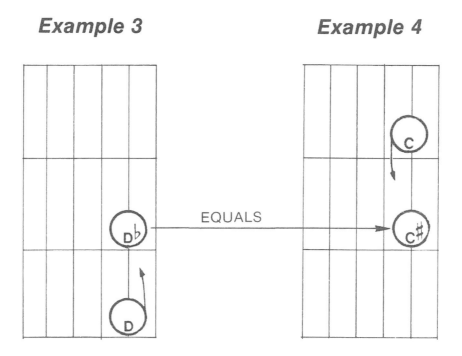

In example 3 D♭ is on the 2nd fret of the 2nd string.

In example 4 C♯ is on the 2nd fret of the 2nd string.

Conclusion

D♭ and C♯ are the same note (2nd fret, 2nd string) with different names.

RULE: A flat is the same note as the sharp that is alphabetically before it. Therefore, B♭ is the same as A♯ - A comes before B in the alphabet. D♭ is the same as C♯ - C comes before D in the alphabet E♭ is the same as D♯ - D comes before E in the alphabet.

You will be given more of an opportunity to practice the application of this rule in the following pages.

A CHORD FORM

1) **A chord form** is a **fixed arrangement of fingers** that must be **played on particular strings.**

2) You have learned your musical alphabet on the previous pages. The symbol for the particular chord form will be placed next to the letter in the musical alphabet.

3) The four chord forms you will learn, and the symbols that represent them, are shown on the following table.

4) The alphabetical name of a particular form is determined by the fret upon which it is played. Therefore, if the minor form is played on the 5th fret, it is an A minor (Am). If the same form is played on the 7th fret, it is a B minor (Bm).

Chord Form	Symbol	Example
Minor	M	A^M (A Minor)
Minor Seventh	M7	$B{\sharp}^{M7}$ (B sharp Minor Seventh)
Seventh	7	D^7 (D Seventh)
Major	No symbol indicates a major chord	A (A Major)

In other words, a minor, minor seventh, seventh or major form will remain a minor, minor seventh, seventh, or major form even though its **alphabetical name will be determined by the fret upon which it is played.**

5) We will now study the minor in detail on the next page.

THE MINOR FORM (m)

1) When (m) is placed next to a letter, a minor chord should be played.

2) At this point we will use your knowledge of both the musical alphabet and of sharps and flats.

3) The alphabetical name of the minor form is determined by the fret number it is played upon.

4) The advantage of using this and other bar forms is that they may be moved up and down the neck of the guitar. As they are moved up and down the neck of the guitar, they assume different names depending on the fret they are played on.

Student Notes

THE MINOR FORM

(Explanation of sharp and flat charts on the following page)

1) The sharp and flat charts are a visual representation of the minor form being moved up and down the neck of the guitar.

2) As you can see, the same form (the minor form) takes on various names as it is moved up and down the neck of the guitar.

3) **This chart was not made to be memorized.** Instead it is here to show you how your musical alphabet works in relation to the minor bar form.

4) The sharp chart shows you the minor form as it starts on the 1st fret, and is moved up the neck of the guitar.

5) The flat chart shows you the minor form as it starts on the 13th fret, and is moved down the neck of the guitar.

6) On both charts the minor form, which is played on the 1st fret, is called Fm.

7) **On the 2nd fret** the **minor form** takes on **two different names even though it is the same chord.**

8) On the 2nd fret of the guitar, the minor form is called either G$^\flat$m or F$^\sharp$m. **(Remember the rule that a flat equals the sharp that is alphabetically before it).**

9) On the 4th fret the minor form is called either A$^\flat$m or G$^\sharp$m.

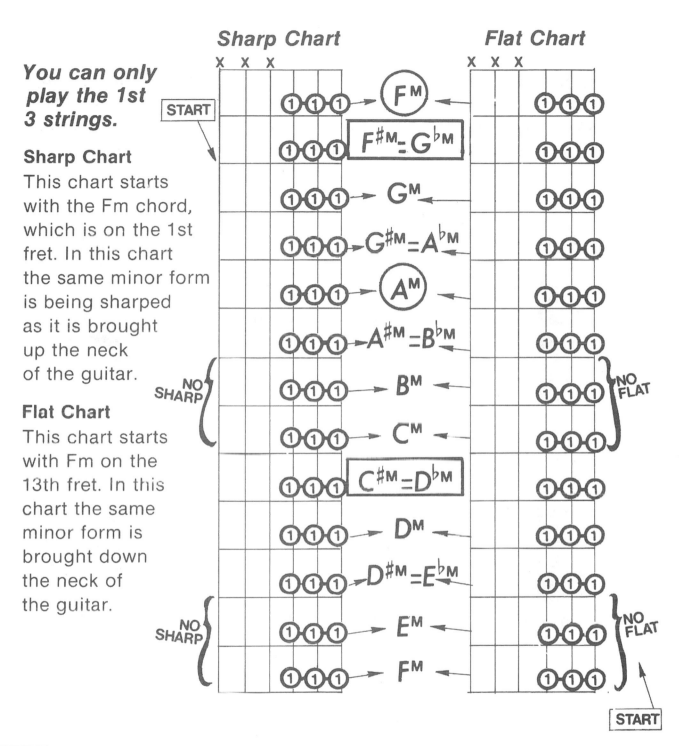

You can only play the 1st 3 strings.

Sharp Chart

This chart starts with the Fm chord, which is on the 1st fret. In this chart the same minor form is being sharped as it is brought up the neck of the guitar.

Flat Chart

This chart starts with Fm on the 13th fret. In this chart the same minor form is brought down the neck of the guitar.

Sharp Chart   **Flat Chart**

F^M

F#M=GbM

G^M

G#M=AbM

A^M

A#M=BbM

B^M

C^M

C#M=DbM

D^M

D#M=EbM

E^M

F^M

START

NO SHARP   NO FLAT

NO SHARP   NO FLAT

START

F#m=Gbm — As you can see on this fret (2nd fret), this chord may be called either F#m or Gbm. **F#m and Gbm are the same chord, same position, with different names.**

C#m=Dbm — C#m and Dbm are the same chord.

(Fm) On the 1st fret this chord position has only one name, Fm.

(Am) On the 5th fret this chord position has only one name, Am.

THE MINOR FORM

Below is a photographic chart of the minor form. It is important to note that **between the notes E and F and B and C, you do not skip a fret.** In other words when moving a chord up or down the neck of the guitar, there is a sharp and flat between every note except B and C and E and F.

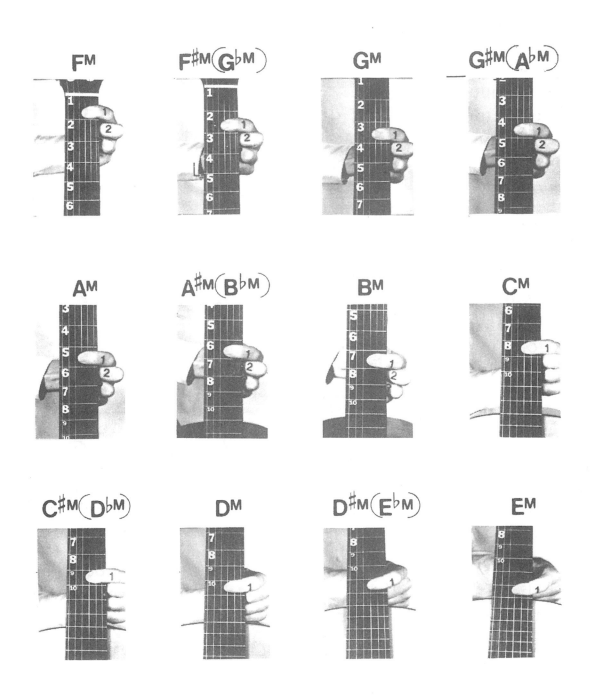

The A Minor (Am) Chord

(m indicates that the minor form will be used)

The first chord we will study is an Am (A minor) chord. **The Am chord is the minor form placed on the 5th fret.** (see sharp and flat charts page). We will study the Am and try to play it until you get a clear sound. If you can play the Am clearly, you will be able to play the minor form on any fret on the guitar and get a clear sound.

To play Am you must press down with your **1st finger** on the **5th fret** of the **1st, 2nd,** and **3rd strings.**

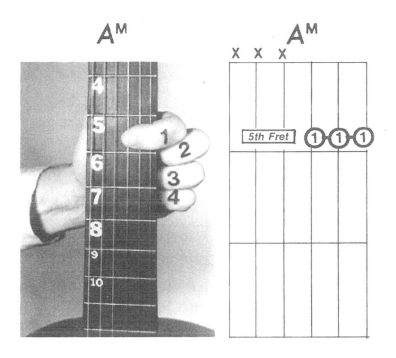

You should only play the 1st, 2nd and 3rd strings. Practice this chord until all strings make a clear sound. Remember to press firmly with your thumb on the back of the guitar.

THE MAJOR FORM

The major form may also be moved up and down the neck of the guitar. The name of the chord is determined by which fret it is played upon.

The major form is shown below on various frets of the guitar. The photo of the form is directly below the guitar diagram.

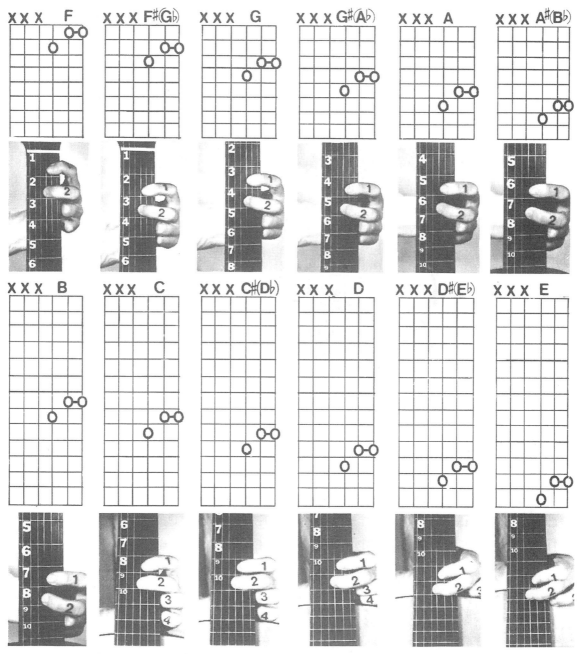

On the 5th fret this chord is an A. A letter with no other symbol represents a major chord. A is the same as A major.

On the 6th fret this chord's name is either A♯ or B♭

The A Major Chord (A)

The first chord we will study is A major (A). **The A Chord** is simply a **major form placed on the 5th fret.** To play this chord you must press down with your **1st finger** on the **5th fret** of the **1st and 2nd strings.** Your **2nd finger** should be on the **6th fret** of the **3rd string.**

You should only play the 1st three strings.

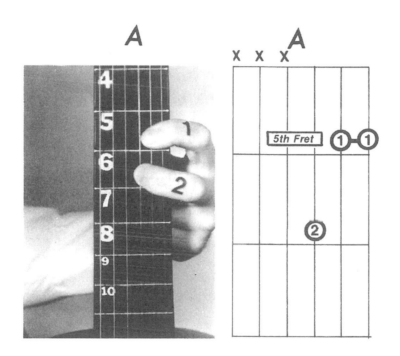

Practice and learn this chord until all three strings make a clear sound.

THE SEVENTH FORM (7)

((7) is the symbol for the seventh form)

1) The seventh form is shown below on various frets of the guitar. The alphabetical name of this form will be determined by which fret it is played upon.

2) If you learn the name of one of the seventh chords, you could figure out the names of all the seventh chords by using the musical alphabet.

3) On the next page a list is provided of seventh chord forms with their names as played on the various frets of the guitar. Some of the names have been left blank. Using your musical alphabet, see if you can fill in the blanks.

Student Notes

THE SEVENTH FORM (7)

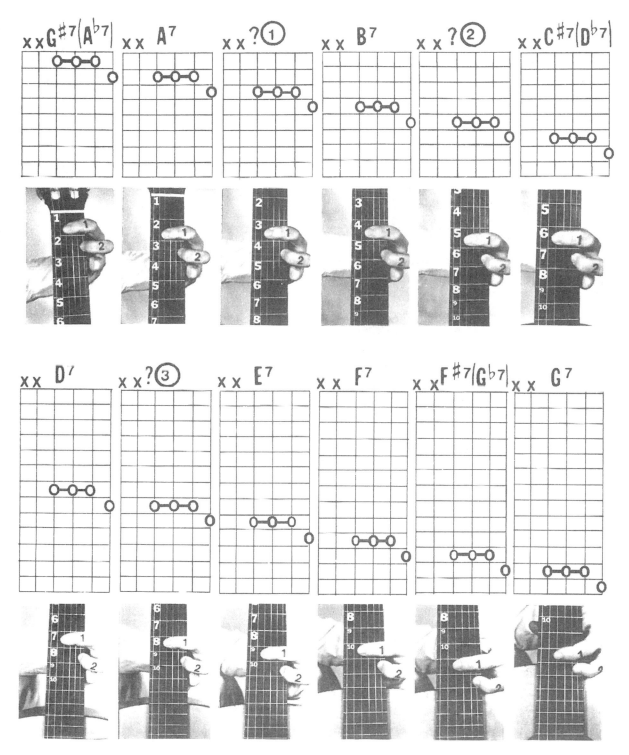

ANSWERS

(No sharps between B & C)

① A#7(Bb7) ② C7 ③ D#7/Eb7

The C Seventh Chord (C7)

The first seventh chord we will study will be the C7 chord. The C7 is the seventh form placed on the 5th fret. To play **C7,** you must press down with your **1st finger** on the **5th fret** on the **2nd, 3rd, and 4th strings.** Your **2nd finger** should be on the **6th fret** of the **1st string.**

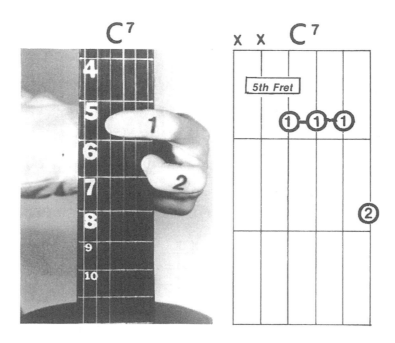

You should only play the 1st four strings. Each string should have a clear sound.

PRACTICE WITH OUR MAJOR, MINOR AND SEVENTH BAR CHORDS

You should be able to play all these songs clearly before going on. Remember, only strike the strings that your fingers are on. These are familiar songs.

How to play the following songs using chords.

1) The tunes on the following pages have only the words and chords marked in.

2) While playing these tunes, you should sing the melodies as you play the chords. **(It doesn't matter how bad your voice is, you are doing this to practice chord changing.)**

3) There are no marks to indicate how many times you play each chord. The marks are left out in order to avoid confusion. Play the chords using any strum you choose. **(Change chords when you see the chord change on top of the word.**

4) You shouldn't worry about how many times you strike each chord. You should **only be concerned** about **changing from one chord to another without stopping** and **getting a clear sound** from each chord you play.

ROW YOUR BOAT

G ⇨
Row, row, row your boat, Gently down the stream -

                                                  D⁷ ⇨   **G** ⇨
Merrily, merrily, merrily, merrily, Life is but a dream. -

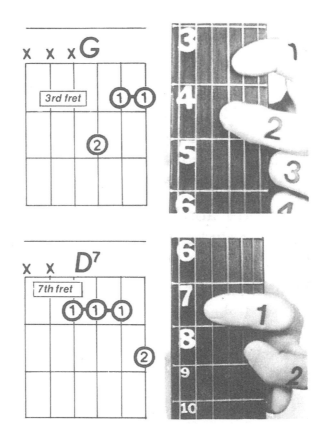

Make sure you play the chord positions on the correct fret. Are you getting a clear sound? Can you change from one chord to another without stopping your strum?

THE OLD GRAY MARE

G ⇨
Oh, the Old Gray Mare, she ain't what she used to be,

D ⇨   **G** ⇨
Ain't what she used to be, Ain't what she used to be, The Old Gray

                                    D ⇨   **G** ⇨
Mare, she ain't what she used to be, Many long years a - go.

G ⇨   **C** ⇨ · **G** ⇨
Man - y long years a - go, Man - y long years a - go, Oh! The Old

                                    D ⇨   **G** ⇨
Gray Mare, she ain't what she used to be, Man - y long years a - go.

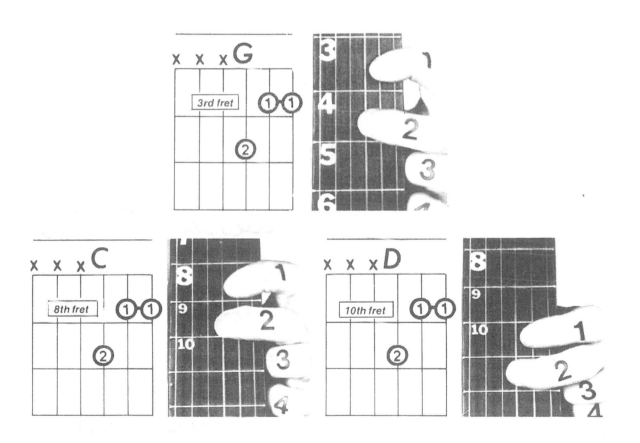

DOWN BY THE RIVERSIDE

G ⇨
I'm gonna lay down my sword and shield,

           D⁷ ⇨   **G** ⇨
Down by the riverside, down by the riverside, down by the riverside,

I'm gonna lay down my sword and shield,

           D⁷ ⇨   **G** ⇨
Down by the riverside and study war no more.

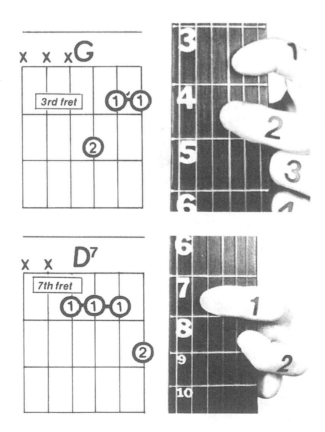

HAVA NAGILAH

G ⇨
Ha - va _____ Na - gi - lah,   Ha - va _____ Na - gi - lah,

C^M ⇨   **G** ⇨
Ha - va _____ Na - gi - lah,   vay - nis _____ m' chayh,

G ⇨
Ha - vah _____ Na - gi - lah   Ha - vah _____ Na - gi - lah,

C^M ⇨   **G** ⇨
Ha - vah _____ Na - gi - lah,   vay - nis _____ m' chayh.

G ⇨   **F^M** ⇨
Hav - ah n' ra - ne - nah, ha - vah n' ra - ne - nah,

F^M ⇨   **G** ⇨
Ha - vah n' ra - ne - nah, vay - nis _____ m' - chayh. Ha - vah n'

                F^M ⇨
ra - ne - nah, ha - vah n' - ra - ne - nah, ha - vah n' - ra - ne - nah,

G ⇨
vay - nis _____ m' - chayh.

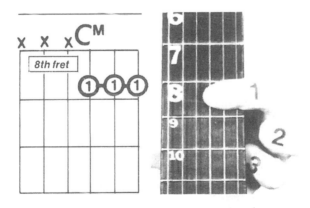

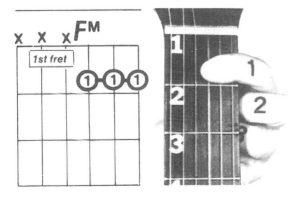

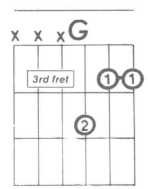

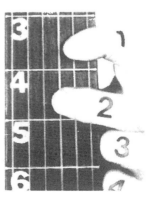

FOR HE'S A JOLLY GOOD FELLOW

A➡
For he's a jol - ly good fel - low, for he's a jol - ly good fel - low, *(E7➡)* *(A➡)*

D➡   A➡   E7➡ A➡
For he's a jol - ly good fel - low, That no - body can de - ny._____

D➡   A➡   D➡   A➡
Which no - body can de - ny _____ which no - body can de - ny,

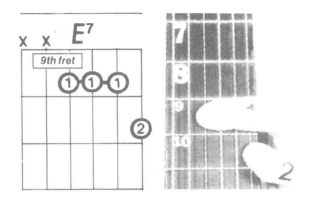

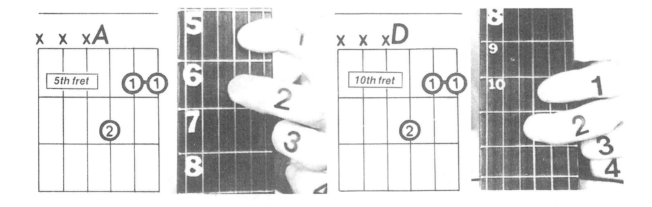

I'VE BEEN WORKING ON THE RAILROAD

G⇨
I've been work-ing on the rail - road, C⇨ All the live long G⇨ day

G⇨
I've been working on the rail - road, Just to A⁷⇨ pass the time a - D⁷⇨ way

D⁷⇨
Don't you hear the whis-tle blow - ing, G⇨ Rise up so C⇨ ear-ly in the B⁷⇨ morn;

C⇨
Can't you hear the cap-tain shout in' G⇨ __ Din - ah D⁷⇨ blow your G⇨ horn.

x x x **C**

8th fret ① ①
②

x x **B⁷**

4th fret ① ① ①
②

x x x **G**

3rd fret ① ①
②

x x **A⁷**

2nd fret ① ① ①
②

x x **D⁷**

7th fret ① ① ①
②

THE MINOR SEVENTH FORM (m7)

The minor seventh form, like the other forms we have learned, may be placed on any of the frets of the guitar. We will study the minor seventh form on the 5th fret. When played on the 5th fret, this form is an Am7.

To play **Am7** (minor seventh) you should press down with your **1st finger** on the **5th fret** of the **1st, 2nd 3rd and 4th strings.** You should only play the four strings that your finger is on.

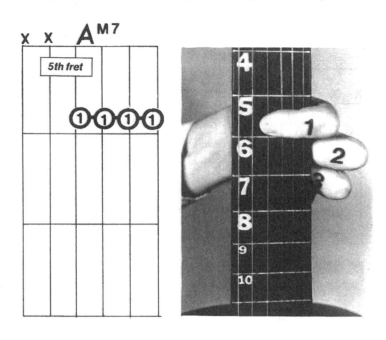

1) What would this chord be on the 6th fret?

2) What would it be on the 4th fret?

3) What would this be on the 3rd fret?

4) What would this be on the 7th fret?

Answers

1) A#m7(Bbm7)   2) G#m7(Abm7)   3) Gm7   4) Bm7

THE FULL BAR FORM

The bar chords we have learned so far have limited us to the playing of only those strings that we put our fingers on. The advantage of using the full bar chord is that it allows us to play on all six strings. By playing all six strings the chord sounds noticeably more powerful and full.

Developing the Full Bar Form

Many **full bar forms** are **extensions** of simple **1st position chords.** (1st position chords are chords that are played on the 1st three frets of the guitar).

Chart of 1st position major form

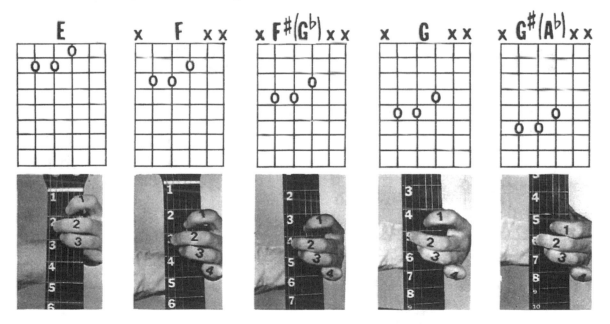

In the above diagram you can see a first position major form being moved down the neck of the guitar. The problem with using this form is that, except for the E chord (as the x's indicates), you can only play the 3rd, 4th and 5th strings. Being able to play only the middle strings would make the use of this chord form difficult.

THE FULL MAJOR BAR FORM

By placing your 1st finger across the six strings you change the 1st position major form into a full bar form.

Chart of Full Major Bar Form

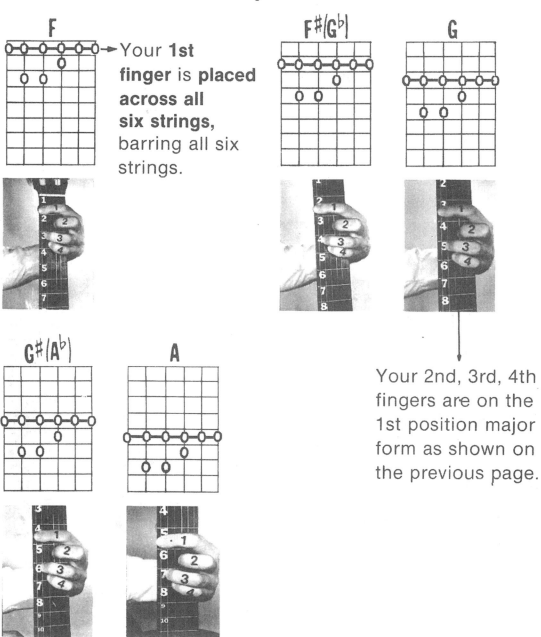

→ Your **1st finger** is **placed across all six strings,** barring all six strings.

Your 2nd, 3rd, 4th fingers are on the 1st position major form as shown on the previous page.

The full bar forms, like our other bar forms, will acquire different alphabetical names depending on what fret they are played on the guitar. Once again, you can figure out the various names of the forms by using your musical alphabet.

The A Major Chord (A)

We will study the full bar form on the 5th fret. The full bar form as played on the 5th fret is an A major chord (A).

You must be thinking, **"How am I ever going to press down all six strings with one finger?"** It's really not as hard as it looks. Here are some helpful hints.

To play an **A** your **1st finger** must **bar all six strings** on the **5th fret.** Your **2nd finger** should be on the **6th fret** of the **3rd string.** Your **3rd finger** should be on the **7th fret** of the **5th string** and your **4th finger** should be on the **7th fret** of the **4th string.**

The Right Way

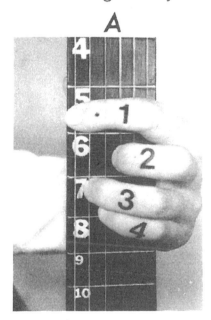

The Wrong Way

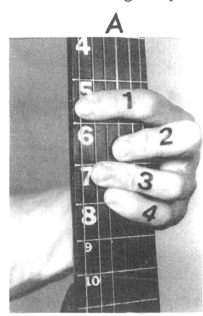

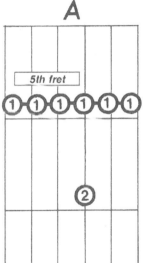

Your fingers should be up straight. If you bend your fingers over, you will get a thud or unclear sounds.

Your fingers are bent over touching other strings causing unclear sounds.

The A Major Chord

A great deal of time should be spent on this particular chord. As soon as you can play this chord, the other bar chords will be much easier to play.

Pressure Points for the A Chord

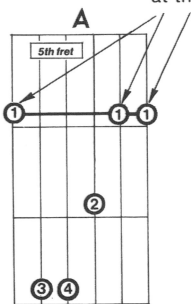

Pressure from your 1st finger should be directed at these points.

1) You should press down on all 6 strings with your 1st finger.

2) As you can see from the diagram above, you really only have to concentrate on pressing down with your 1st finger on the 1st, 2nd and 6th strings.

3) You should apply pressure with your 2nd, 3rd and 4th fingers on the 3rd, 4th and 5th strings.

MUSICAL PROGRESSIONS

We will practice our full bar form using two very common musical progressions. **A chord progression** is a **pattern of chords** that is **used over and over again.**

There are a great many musical progressions. Two progressions have been chosen which are common to many of the popular songs that are heard on the radio.

The strum pattern we will use is ⊓ ⊓ ᴠᴠ ⊓ (down, down, up up, down). You should repeat this progression until your full bar chords sound clear, and you can change them with ease.

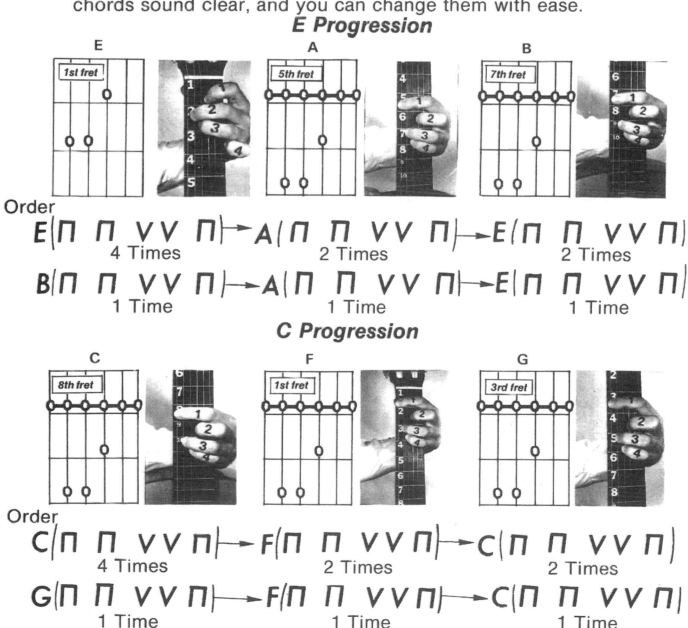

E Progression

E   A   B

Order

E(⊓ ⊓ ᴠ ᴠ ⊓) → A(⊓ ⊓ ᴠ ᴠ ⊓) → E(⊓ ⊓ ᴠ ᴠ ⊓)
4 Times   2 Times   2 Times

B(⊓ ⊓ ᴠ ᴠ ⊓) → A(⊓ ⊓ ᴠ ᴠ ⊓) → E(⊓ ⊓ ᴠ ᴠ ⊓)
1 Time   1 Time   1 Time

C Progression

C   F   G

Order

C(⊓ ⊓ ᴠ ᴠ ⊓) → F(⊓ ⊓ ᴠ ᴠ ⊓) → C(⊓ ⊓ ᴠ ᴠ ⊓)
4 Times   2 Times   2 Times

G(⊓ ⊓ ᴠ ᴠ ⊓) → F(⊓ ⊓ ᴠ ᴠ ⊓) → C(⊓ ⊓ ᴠ ᴠ ⊓)
1 Time   1 Time   1 Time

VARIATIONS OF THE MAJOR BAR FORM

By merely adding fingers to or subtracting fingers from the bar you have just learned, you can play three variations of that bar form which are the most commonly used chords in popular music.

As we have already stated, full bar forms are, for the most part, extentions of simple 1st position chords.

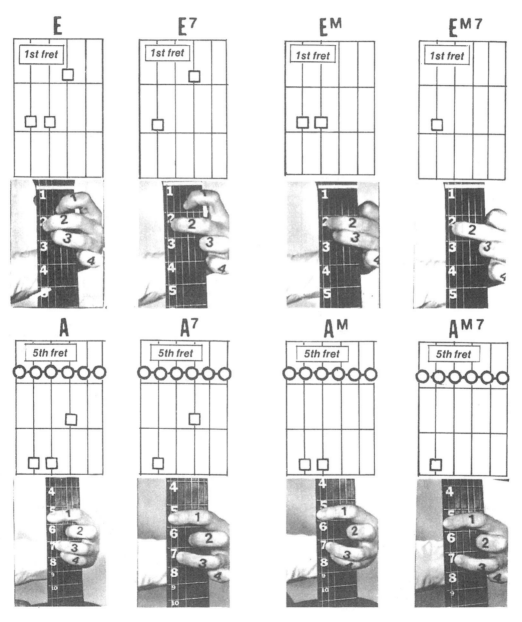

In each of the above diagrams the 1st position chords (E, E7, Em, Em7) are brought up the neck of the guitar, and a bar (which is your 1st finger) is placed across the 5th fret. The finger position of the 1st position chords are represented by rectangles on the diagrams. The bar position is represented by the circles.

VARIATIONS OF THE MAJOR BAR FORM

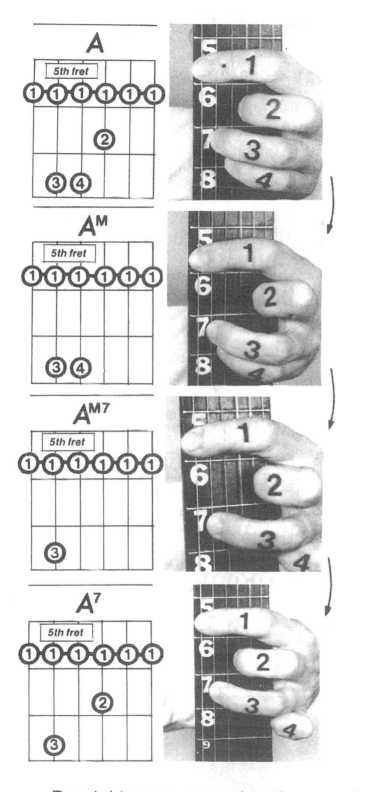

1) To change from A to Am simply lift up your 2nd finger.

2) To change from Am to Am7 simply lift up your 4th finger.

3) To change from Am7 to A7 simply put your 2nd finger on the 6th fret of the 3rd string.

By picking up or putting down various fingers, you can change this bar into four chord forms. You can increase the number of chords you can play by moving these forms up and down the neck of the guitar.

Practice Using Full Bar Chords

1) Use the following songs in order to practice the full bar chords you have learned.

2) Make sure that you are playing the bar form on the correct fret.

3) **Practice** these songs **until** you can play these chords clearly and **change from one chord to another smoothly.**

4) It takes a good deal of practice to get the feel of these chords. If you can master the following songs, you should be able to play any bar form in any song.

MARINE'S HYMN

D⇨   A⁷⇨   D⇩
From the Halls of Mon - te - zu _____ ma To the shores of Trip-o-li; _

D⇨   A⁷⇨   D⇨
We _____ fight our coun- try's bat - tles, on the land and on the sea.

D⇨ G⇨   D⇨   G⇨   D⇨
First to fight for right and free - dom And to keep our hon-or clean;

D⇨   A⁷⇨   D⇨
We are proud to claim the ti - tle of U - nit - ed States Mar-ines. __

SWANEE RIVER

C⇨   F⇨   C⇨
Way down up - on the Swa - nee River, Far,

G⇨   C⇨
far, a - way, _____ There's where my heart is

F⇨   C⇨   G⇨   C⇨
turn - ing ever, There's where the old folks stay. _____

G⇨   C⇨   F⇨
All the world is sad and drea - ry, Ev' - ry

C⇨   F⇨
where I roam, _____ Oh, dar - kies how my heart grows

C⇨   G⇨   C⇨
wea-ry, Far from the old folks at home.

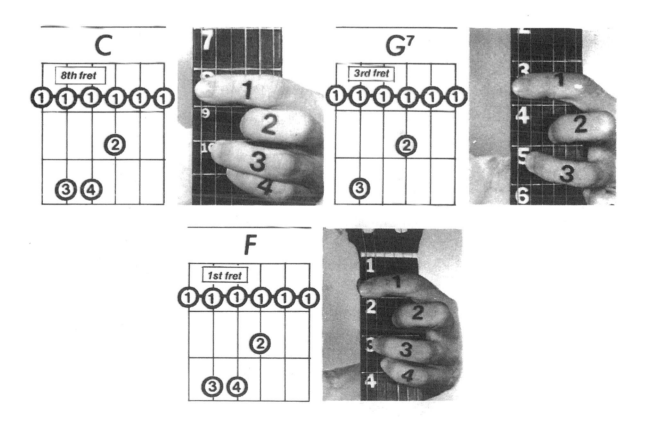

SWING LOW, SWEET CHARIOT

G➡   C➡   G➡
Swing Low, Sweet Char - i - ot, _____ Com - in' for to car-ry me

D➡ G➡   C➡
home. Swing_____Low, Sweet Char - i - ot, _____

C➡   G➡   C➡
Com - in' for to car - ry me home. Looked o - ver Jor - dan,

A⁷➡   G➡   D➡
What did I see? _____ com - in' for to car - ry me home? A

G➡   C➡   G➡   C➡
band _____ of an - gels com-in' af-ter me, _____ Com-in' for to

D➡   G➡
car-ry me home!

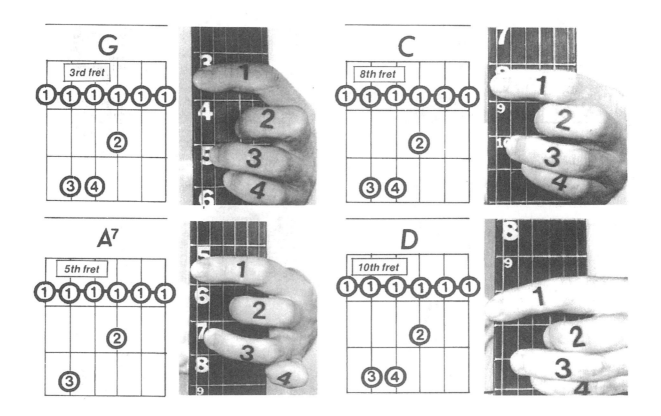

DECK THE HALLS

F⇨   C⇨   F⇨ C⇨ F⇨
Deck the halls with boughs of hol - ly, Fa la la la la, la la la la,

F⇨   C⇨   F⇨ C⇨ F⇨
'Tis the sea-son to be jol-ly, Fa la la la la, la la la la,

C⁷⇨   F⇨   B♭⇨   G⁷⇨ C⇨
Don we now our gay ap - par - el, Fa la la, La la la, La la la.

F⇨   B♭⇨   F⇨ C⇨ F⇨
Troll an an - cient Yule-tide car - ol, Fa la la la la, La la la la.

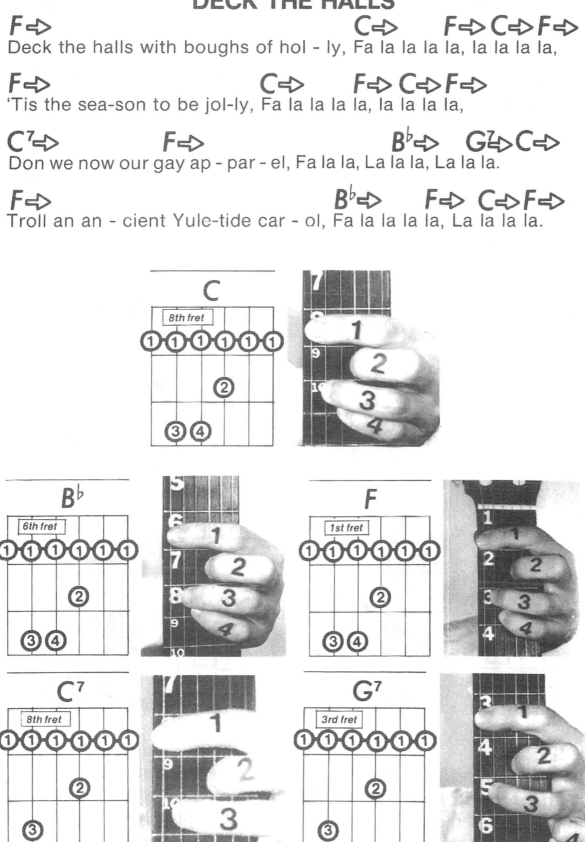

ANOTHER MINOR AND MINOR 7TH BAR FORM

Although you have already learned to play minor and minor seventh chords using one bar form, it is **important** that **you learn more than one full bar form** so you **won't have to jump all over the neck of the guitar** to find a particular chord. This will become clearer when you play the last group of songs.

Chart of 1st Position Minor and Minor Seventh Chords

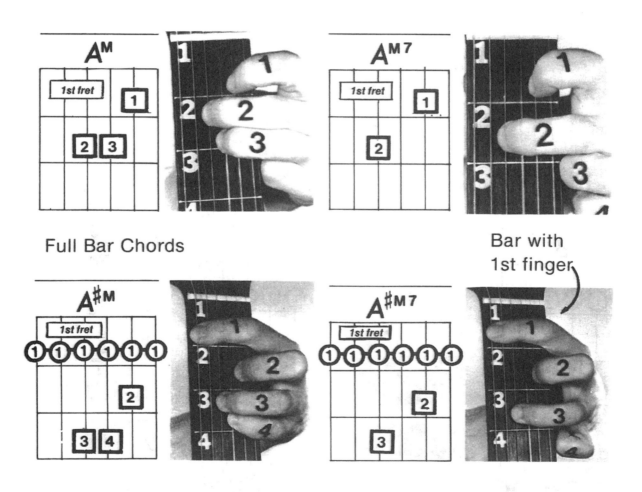

Full Bar Chords

Bar with
1st finger

As you bring the 1st position chords up one fret, they become sharped. In order to play all the strings you must place your 1st finger across the entire six strings on the 1st fret. Once you have barred the 1st fret with your 1st finger, you may move the chord form up the neck of the guitar, its name will depend on the fret it is on.

The D Minor (Dm)
And D Minor Seventh (Dm7) Chords

The minor and minor 7th forms are placed on the 5th fret where they become Dm and Dm7.

To play **Dm** your **1st finger** should bar (press down) **all six strings** on the **5th fret.** Your **2nd finger** should be on the **6th fret** of the **2nd string.** Your **3rd finger** should be on the **7th fret** of the **4th string,** and your **4th finger** should be on the **7th fret** of the **3rd string.**

To play **Dm7, remove** the **4th finger** from the **Dm chord.**

Pressure from your 1st finger should be directed at these points.

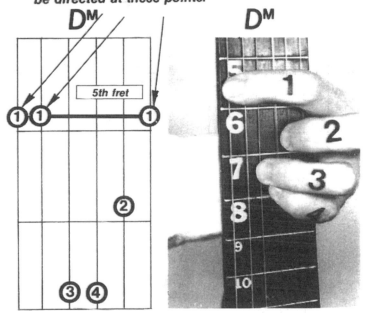

Pressure from your 1st finger should be directed at these points.

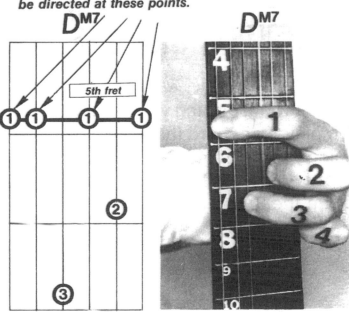

ANOTHER FULL MAJOR BAR FORM

This full bar form is the most difficult for most people to play and will take a great deal of practice and patience to master.

1st Position Chord

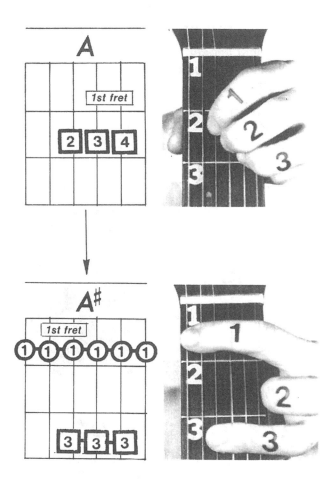

As with the minor form, placing your 1st finger across the 1st fret gives you a complete bar chord that may be moved up the neck of the guitar. Placing your 1st finger across the 1st fret and moving the 1st position chord down one fret changes the chord to A#. A# is a full bar chord. On the 3rd fret this form is a C chord.

THE D MAJOR (D) CHORD

To play **D** your **1st finger** must **bar** (press down) **all six strings** on the **5th fret.** Your **3rd finger** should **bar** the **2nd, 3rd** and **4th strings** on the **7th fret.**

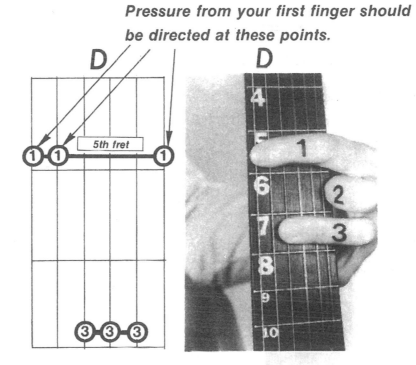

Pressure from your first finger should be directed at these points.

This bar position is the most difficult for most people. With time and practice you will be able to play this chord.

PRACTICE USING ALL THE FULL BAR FORMS
WE HAVE LEARNED

THIS TRAIN

G⇨   Aᴹ⇨   D⇨   G⇨

This train is bound for glo - ry, this train, _____

G⇨   D⇨   G⇨

This train is bound for glo - ry, this train, _____ This train is

G⇨   Aᴹ⇨   Eᴹ⇨   D⇨

bound for glo - ry, Don't ride none but the good and ho - ly, This

G⇨   Aᴹ⇨   D⇨   G⇨

train is bound for glo - ry, this train. _____

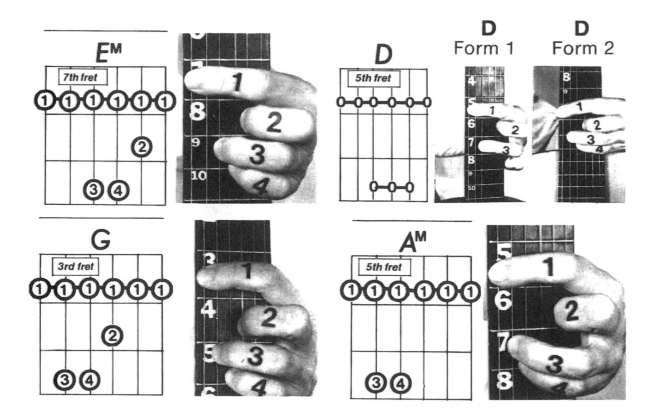

As you can see, it is easier to play D (form 1) than D (form 2) because D (form 1) is closer to the other chords being used. Am is on the 5th fret, and G is on the 3rd fret so it's easier to use the D on the 5th fret.

Since both D's are the **same chord** and **have the same sound**, it **makes more sense** to **use the D** on the **third fret** since you **don't have to move your hand as much.**

THE BATTLE HYMN OF THE REPUBLIC

D ⇨
Mine eyes have seen the glo - ry of the com - ing of the

D ⇨   **G** ⇨
Lord, He is tram - pling out the vin - tage where the

D ⇨
grapes of wrath are stored. He hath loosed the fate - ful

D ⇨   **G** ⇨
light - ning of His ter - ri - ble swift sword, His truth

    A⁷ ⇨   **D** ⇨
is march - ing on.

Refrain:

D ⇨   **G** ⇨
Glo - ry, glo - ry, hal - le - lu - jah! Glo - ry,

      D ⇨
Glo - ry, hal - le - lu - jah! Glo - ry, Glo - ry, hal -

     Eᴹ ⇨ **A⁷** ⇨   **D** ⇨
le - lu - jah! His truth is march - ing on.

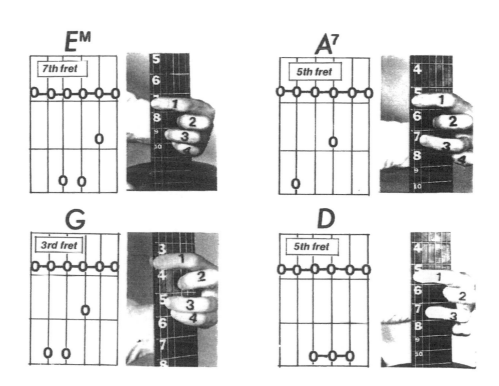

BAND PLAYED ON

C ⇨
Ca - sey would waltz with a straw - ber - ry blonde, and the

G⁷ ⇨
band played on, _____ He'd glide 'cross the floor with the

G⁷ ⇨   **C** ⇨
girl he a - dored, and the band played on, _____ But his

C ⇨   **G⁷** ⇨   **C⁷** ⇨   **F** ⇨   **A⁷** ⇨
brain was so load-ed it near-ly explo - ded, the poor girl would

A⁷ ⇨   **Dᴹ** ⇨   **F** ⇨
shake with a - larm. _____ He'd ne'er leave the girl with the

C ⇨   **D⁷** ⇨ **G⁷** ⇨ **C** ⇨
straw-ber-ry curls, and the band played on. _____

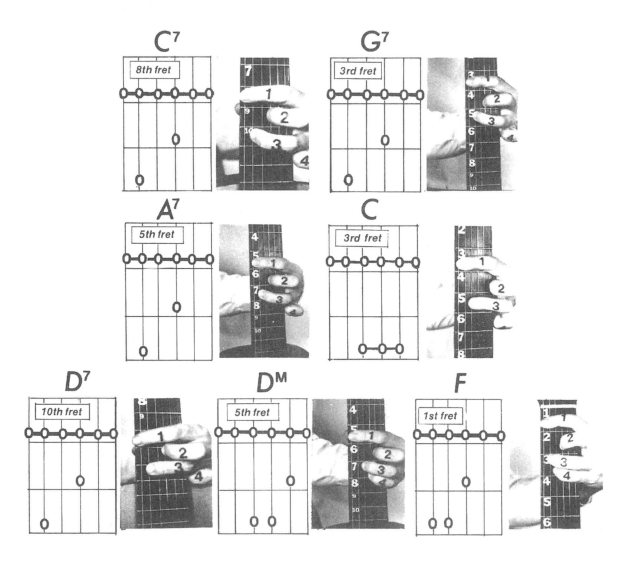

BICYCLE BUILT FOR TWO

C→   F→
Dai - sy, Dai - sy, Give me your an - swer

C→   G⁷→ C→   D→
do, _____ I'm half cra - zy, All for the

D→ G⁷→   C→
love of you, _____ It won't be a styl - ish mar - riage! _____

C→   F→ C→
I can't af - ford a car-riage, _____ But you'll look

G⁷→   C→ G⁷→   C→   G⁷→ C→
sweet up - on the seat of a bi - cy - cle built for two. _____

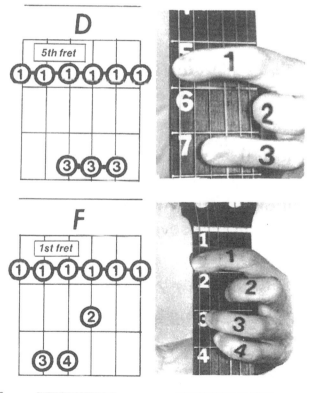

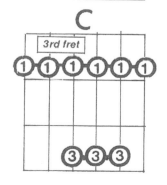

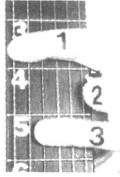

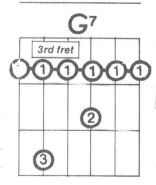

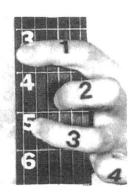

HOW TO CHANGE THE CHORDS OF A SONG TO ACCOMPANY YOUR VOICE
(Changing the Key)

Often when you buy sheet music to your favorite songs it is written in a key which is either too high or too low for your voice. **Making the chords higher or lower** so that you can sing along with your favorite songs **is called changing the key.**

Strumming the chords to a song is called playing the rhythm. Singing the words to a song is called singing the melody.

Though the rhythm and melody remain the same when you change the key of a song, the chords are played either higher or lower making it easier for you to sing the song as you play those chords.

General Rules for using the Changing Key Chart

1) The **changing key chart** on the following page **lists only the major chords** and their **sharps and flats.**

2) When **changing the key,** the **1st letter of the chord** is the **only thing that changes.** This is represented on the chart. However, a minor (m), a minor seventh (m7) or a seventh (7), etc., remains a minor, minor seventh or a seventh, etc., though its alphabetical name is different.

3) You can change to any key you want.

4) If you want to **make the song higher,** you should **add to your first chord.**

5) If you **want to make the song lower,** you should **subtract from your first chord.**

6) Once you have decided how much to add to or subtract from the first chord, then you **must add or subtract** that **same number from all the chords in the song.**

7) If you look at the examples that follow, this will not appear as complicated as it seems.

Key Change Chart

Higher ———→

A	A#	B	C	C#	D	D#	E	F	F#	G	G#	A	A#	B	C	C#	D	D#	E	F	F#	G	G#	A
1	2	3	4	5	6	7	8	9	10	11	12	13	14	15	16	17	18	19	20	21	22	23	24	25
A	B♭	B	C	D♭	D	E♭	E	F	G♭	G	A♭	A	B♭	B	C	D♭	D	E♭	E	F	G♭	G	A♭	A

———→

←——— **Lower**

Change 1
from C to D
would be +2

Making a Song Higher

1) To make a song higher you should start at your 1st chord and go in the direction of the arrow (to the right). The farther you go on the chart the higher the song. (**Changing from a C (4 on the chart) to G (12) makes the song higher than changing from C(4) to E(8).**

2) It doesn't matter where you start on the chart. You could start on C(4) or C(16) and still have the same results.

CHANGE NUMBER 1

Key Change Chart

Higher ⟶

A	A♯	B	C	C♯	D	D♯	E	F	F♯	G	G♯	A	A♯	B	C	C♯	D	D♯	E	F	F♯	G	G♯	A
1	2	3	4	5	6	7	8	9	10	11	12	13	14	15	16	17	18	19	20	21	22	23	24	25
A	B♭	B	C	D♭	D	E♭	E	F	G♭	G	A♭	A	B♭	B	C	D♭	D	E♭	E	F	G♭	G	A♭	A

⟵ Lower

1) Assume the song you want to make higher has only 4 chords in it: C, E7, Am and Em7.

2) You should start on the 1st chord C and make the song a little higher. (Remember, we could move the chord up as many steps as we want).

3) Let's move the C chord up to D.

4) You can see that **moving** the **chord** from **C** to **D** would be a **plus 2 on the chart.**

5) You should now **add 2** to **each** of the **other chords in the song.**

6) **E7 becomes F♯7.** Remember, you should only look for E on the chart. The seventh (7) does not change. Only the 1st letter of the chord changes.

7) **Am becomes Bm.** A is 1 on the chart. If you add 2, you get 3 which is B on the chart. If you use the A that is 13 on the chart and added 2, you get 15 which is still B on the chart.

8) **Em7 becomes F♯m7**

9) Our new song is a little higher. Look below to see the change.

1st Version   C, E7, Am Em7

2nd Version   D, F♯7, Bm F♯m7 - This has the same melody as the 1st song, but a little higher.

Making a Song Lower

Key Change Chart

Higher ──────→

A	A#	B	C	C#	D	D#	E	F	F#	G	G#	A	A#	B	C	C#	D	D#	E	F	F#	G	G#	A
1	2	3	4	5	6	7	8	9	10	11	12	13	14	15	16	17	18	19	20	21	22	23	24	25
A	B♭	B	C	D♭	D	E♭	E	F	G♭	G	A♭	A	B♭	B	C	D♭	D	E♭	E	F	G♭	G	A♭	A

←────── Lower

Change 2

1) This is the same chart as on the other page, but placed here for your convenience.

2) Let us say that our song chords are D7, Fm, A#, Bm7.

3) **Our 1st chord, D7,** will be **changed to A7.** This will make the entire song lower.

4) You can see that moving from **D7** to **A7** on our chart would be **minus 5.**

5) You should now have to **subtract 5 from each** of the **other** original **chords in our song.**

6) **Fm** becomes **Cm**. F is 9 on our chart. When you subtract 5, you get 4 which is C on our chart.

7) **A#** becomes **F.**

8) **Bm7** becomes **F# m7.**

9) Now our song is lower.

1st Version	D7, Fm, A#, Bm7
2nd Version	A7, Cm, F, F# m7 - This has the same melody as the 1st version but lower.

Changing Keys
(Conclusion)

1) Only the **1st letter** of the chord **is changed** when **changing keys.**

2) The amount that you change the song depends on how much higher or lower you want to make the song.

3) Regardless of how you decide to change the song (either adding, making the song higher, or subtracting, making the song lower), **you must make the same change on all the chords in the song.** For example, if you add 3 to the first chord, you must add 3 (on the chart) to every chord in the song.

Practice

1)

1st Version   Dm7, E7, A#m, Bm - Find the circled letter on the chart and add 4 to each.

2nd Version ____, ___, ____, ___ - *Make this higher by 4.*

2)

1st Version   Am, A, B, Gm7, D7 - Find the circled letter on the chart and subtract 3 from each.

2nd Version   ___, __, __, ___, __- *Make this lower by 3.*

Answers;

1) F#m7, G#7, Dm, D#m
2) F#m, F#, G#, Em7, B7

A PRACTICE SONG CHANGED INTO 3 KEYS

KUM—BA—YAH

High **F** ➪
(+5)

Middle **C** ➪
(−3)

Low **A** ➪

A♯ ➪ **F** ➪   These numbers
(+5) (+5) ➘ Indicate the plus (+) or
F ➪ **C** ➪   minus (−) you would
(−3) (−3) ➘ add to the middle
D ➪ **A** ➪   chords on your
key change chart.

Kum - Ba - Yah, my Lord! _____ Kum-Ba - Yah! _____ Kum - Ba -

High   **A^M** ➪   **C** ➪   **F** ➪
                      (+5)   (+5)   (+5)

Middle   **E^M** ➪   **G** ➪   **C** ➪
                      (−3)   (−3)   (−3)

Low   **C♯M** ➪   **E** ➪   **A** ➪

Yah, my Lord, _____ Kum - Ba - Yah! _____ Kum - Ba - Yah, my

High   **A♯**➪**F** ➪   **C**➪   **F** ➪
               (+5) (+5)   (+5)   (+5)

Middle   **F**➪**C** ➪   **G**➪   **C**➪
               (−3) (−3)   (−3)   (−3)

Low   **D**➪**A** ➪   **E** ➪   **A** ➪

Lord, _____ Kum - Ba - Yah, _____ Oh Lord! _____ Kum - Ba - Yah!

In the above song we have Kum-Ba-Yah written in 3 keys to suit a high, middle and low voice, The numbers in between the chords represent the change from the key suiting the middle voice on your Key Change Chart. The song can be sung using any one of the three sets of chords depending on your voice. You can change any song that you like using the same procedure given to you on the previous pages.

CHORDS TO KUM-BA-YAH

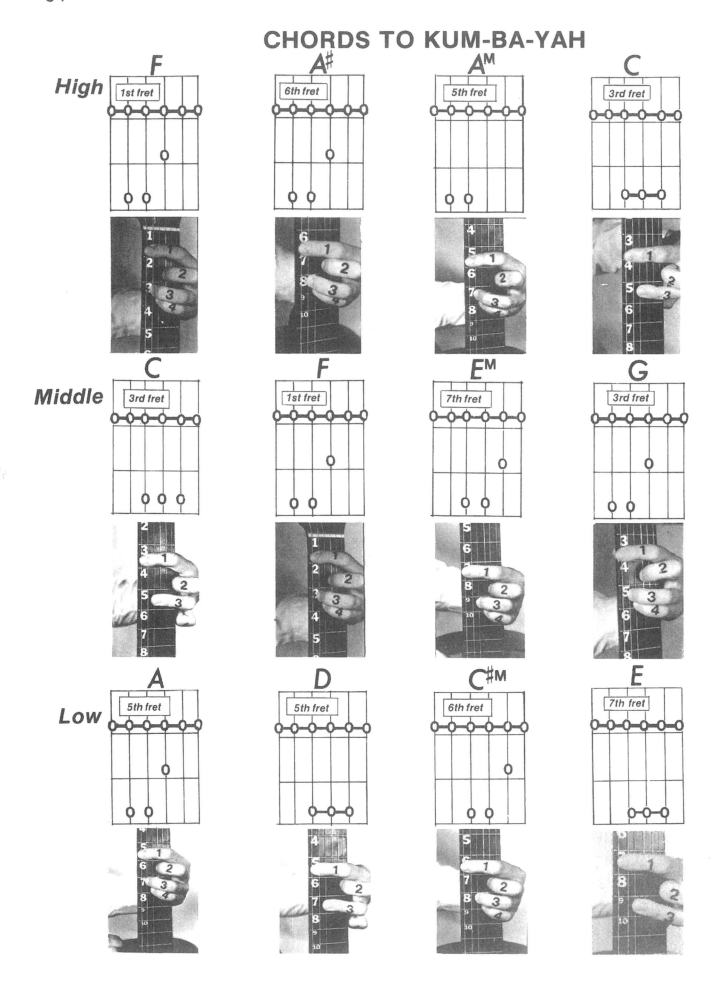

HOW TO FIGURE OUT THE CHORDS TO SONGS SIMPLY BY LISTENING TO THEM
(Playing By Ear)

I have stressed in this book the major, minor, minor 7th, and 7th, chords because they are so widely used in today's modern music.

In order to figure out the chords to a particular song, you must know the names of the notes on the 1st position of the guitar.

1st Position Note Chart

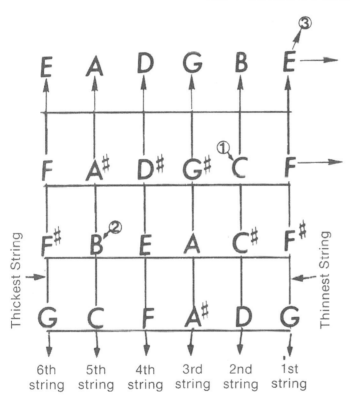

Open

(No fingers down) Striking the string of the guitar with no fingers of your left hand down is called playing the string open.

① If you place your finger on the 1st fret of the 2nd string, the name of the note is C.

② If you place your 2nd finger on the 2nd fret of the 5th string, the name of the note is B.

③ If you strike the 1st string without placing the fingers on your left hand down, you are playing E.

GENERAL RULES FOR USING THE CHORD CHART

1) Find the **1st note in the song** that you are trying to find the chords to.

2) Refer to your **1st position note chart** on the previous page and **find out the name of the note.**

3) **Find the note** on the **note-chord chart,** and you will have **12 possible chords** to choose from. Choose the one that sounds like or goes along with the melody. (Hint: Usually the first chord in a song is a major chord. This means that the 1st chord will probably be one of the first three in the chord column).

4) Once you have determined what the **1st chord** of the song is, continue to **play this chord until** it **no longer sounds correct.**

5) **You must now find a new chord to match** the **change** in the **melody line.** To do this look to the first note of the melody line where the change takes place.

6) Once again, find the note on the note-chord chart, and you will have 12 possible chords to choose from. Choose the one that fits the melody at that point.

7) Once you have found the chord, repeat the same process throughout the entire song.

NOTE-CHORD CHART

Notes

A	A#	B	C	C#	D	D#	E	F	F#	G	G#
A	A#	B	C	C#	D	D#	E	F	F#	G	G#
D	D#	E	F	F#	G	G#	A	A#	B	C	C#
F	F#	G	G#	A	A#	B	C	C#	D	D#	E
A^M	A#^{M}	B^M	C^M	C#^{M}	D^M	D#^{M}	E^M	F^M	F#^{M}	G^M	G#^{M}
D^M	D#^{M}	E^M	F^M	F#^{M}	G^M	G#^{M}	A^M	A#^{M}	B^M	C^M	C#^{M}
A^7	A#^{7}	B^7	C^7	C#^{7}	D^7	D#^{7}	E^7	F^7	F#^{7}	G^7	G#^{7}
B^7	C^7	C#^{7}	D^7	D#^{7}	E^7	F^7	F#^{7}	G^7	G#^{7}	A^7	A#^{7}
D^7	D#^{7}	E^7	F^7	F#^{7}	G^7	G#^{7}	A^7	A#^{7}	B^7	C^7	C#^{7}
F^7	F#^{7}	G^7	G#^{7}	A^7	A#^{7}	B^7	C^7	C#^{7}	D^7	D#^{7}	E^7
A^{M7}	A#^{M7}	B^{M7}	C^{M7}	C#^{M7}	D^{M7}	D#^{M7}	E^{M7}	F^{M7}	F#^{M7}	G^{M7}	G#^{M7}
B^{M7}	C^{M7}	C#^{M7}	D^{M7}	D#^{M7}	E^{M7}	F^{M7}	F#^{M7}	G^{M7}	G#^{M7}	A^{M7}	A#^{M7}
D^{M7}	D#^{M7}	E^{M7}	F^{M7}	F#^{M7}	G^{M7}	G#^{M7}	A^{M7}	A#^{M7}	B^{M7}	C^{M7}	C#^{M7}

Possible Chords for each Note

This chart saves you time because once you find the first note of the song, you have only 12 rather than 12 million variable chords to select from.